MEDITATION

AND MOVEMENT FOR

SELF-HEALING

CATHERINE AYANO NIXON

BALBOA.PRESS
A DIVISION OF HAY HOUSE

Balboa Press books may be ordered through booksellers or by contacting:

Balboa Press
A Division of Hay House
1663 Liberty Drive
Bloomington, IN 47403
www.balboapress.com
844-682-1282

Because of the dynamic nature of the Internet, any web addresses or links contained in this book may have changed since publication and may no longer be valid. The views expressed in this work are solely those of the author and do not necessarily reflect the views of the publisher, and the publisher hereby disclaims any responsibility for them.

The author of this book does not dispense medical advice or prescribe the use of any technique as a form of treatment for physical, emotional, or medical problems without the advice of a physician, either directly or indirectly. The intent of the author is only to offer information of a general nature to help you in your quest for emotional and spiritual well-being. In the event you use any of the information in this book for yourself, which is your constitutional right, the author and the publisher assume no responsibility for your actions.

Any people depicted in stock imagery provided by Getty Images are models, and such images are being used for illustrative purposes only.
Certain stock imagery © Getty Images.

Interior Image Credit: Catherine Ayano Nixon

Print information available on the last page.

ISBN: 978-1-9822-5327-1 (sc)
ISBN: 978-1-9822-5328-8 (e)

Balboa Press rev. date: 11/10/2020

CONTENTS

... Therefore the sage takes care of all people
And abandons no one.
She takes care of all things and abandons nothing...

Lao Tsu, <u>Tao Te Ching</u>

ACKNOWLEDGMENT

Many wonderful people helped me to write this book, including all of my family, particularly my encouraging and supportive parents, James and Yasuko Nixon, who reminded me that I knew what I was doing and that I could draw. Lisa Mathieson and the Lowertown Drawing Circle gave me essential input for the artwork in this book. I also want to thank Jamie Andycha, my supervisor at People Incorporated, who helped me see that I had this knowledge in me. Thank you, William Moyers and Nell Hurley, for helping me to recognize my healing gifts. Thank you to Richard Martin, my SCORE mentor, who helped me to focus on my goals, and to Nancy Beecher, who provided the financial support to bring this book into being. And finally, thank you to a couple of amazing yoga teachers, Tara Sherman and Dec Barry.

PREFACE

In recent years, I had the pleasure of working with individuals who were managing their mental illness or recovery from addictions. They were served by a nonprofit entity in Minneapolis-Saint Paul, Minnesota, U.S.A., called People Incorporated. My job was to lead the clients in meditation, yoga and tai chi as a way to support their wellness. The exercises in this book are some of the simple activities we would do together.

INTRODUCTION

HOW TO USE THIS BOOK

This book is designed to help you learn meditative movement on your own. Of course, it is much more fun to do it with a group. In that case, you will want a designated leader. A person who has prior knowledge of some or most of the information in the book would be an excellent choice for a leader. If your knowledge is about the same, you may want to switch around leaders or have each person study and present a section or exercise to the group. Be creative.

Also, take your time but be steady and consistent with your practice. One exercise at a time is sufficient, one or two times a day. After you have studied the different movements and meditations, it should only take a few minutes to do each exercise. With practice, you will eventually move beyond what is contained in this book but this is a good place to start your meditative movement practice.

The book is written in a way that builds upon each preceding section. That said, you are welcome to move around in the book if that is helpful to you.

There is a drawing for each of the 25 meditative movements in this book. The drawings are approximations meant to give you a sense for how the movement feels in your body and mind. They do not represent an ideal for you to strive to reach. Use the drawings to make notes or color in your experiences with each meditation. Again, be creative. Keep in mind that you may have to try the movements several times before the drawings make sense.

Beneath each drawing is a sentence that describes the energies of the movement with the names, Heaven, Earth, Thunder, Mountain, Wind, Water, Fire and Lake. These sentences are little stories that may help you to feel the movement more intimately. They may stimulate the imagination to add to your meditation and movements. They are not instructions.

The drawing is the drawing. The captions are little stories about the drawings. The movement is your movement. The meditation is your experience.

Know your limits. The movements in this book are fairly simple. However, if standing is too difficult for you, use a chair or make another modification to suit your needs. Much of the meditation in this book is done seated and with hand and arm movements. Even the standing and walking movements can be modified and done in a chair. Also, you certainly do not have to do all of the movements. Focusing on one or two favorites can take you deep into your meditation practice.

Finally, smile and laugh as much as you want. These are healing movements in themselves. Enjoy!

WHAT IS MEDITATION?

Meditation is a process of becoming aware of your thoughts and how they affect your actions and relationships in the world around you. It is a way to slow your mind and your body down and let go of habits and thoughts that are keeping you from being happy and healthy. Meditation leads to self-awareness and self-knowledge. This leads to courage and confidence and the ability to bear with the difficulties of life. It also helps you to enjoy life more fully.

What is meditative movement?

As you practice meditation, you become more aware of how you move in the world; how you walk and talk to others, how you communicate through your actions. Eventually, you can carry the stillness you experience in sitting meditation as you go about your business in the world. You can practice this stillness in action by moving with awareness, paying attention, being mindful.

How is meditation self-healing?

By choosing to meditate, you put your focus on your own self. You care for your own body. You care for your own mind. Your brain, blood, hormones, bones, organs, limbs and skin are all made from the same material and work together to support you in the world. When you put your mind or consciousness on your mind and body, you shine a light on them, just as you do a child or friend in need of attention. That light is love, self-love, and it is healing.

Note: For purposes of this particular meditation guide book, healing does not include "curing" or "fixing" specific diseases, illnesses or structural imbalances in the body. Rather, these meditations can support you emotionally and physically as you go through healing processes with your medical doctors and other health care professionals.

How does this healing look and feel?

You will fall in love with yourself, and possibly the whole universe. This will make you happy. Your thoughts will be happy and as a consequence, your body will be too. A little bit of happiness goes a long way to healing. Does this practice require patience and discipline? Yes. May it take a long time? Perhaps. But when you arrive at your first Aha moment, it'll be easier to persevere. You will begin to look forward to your meditation time as something that brings a spark of joy to your day. Happiness and laughter release healing endorphins and energies in your body. Feeling good is infectious. It helps you and your body to relax and create the conditions for self-healing.

Caution: In the process of moving toward healing, you will most likely come up against the obstacles of negative thought patterns that have interfered in your happiness and health all your life. You may not experience this as pleasant but meditation is a way to face these obstacles, become aware of them and let them go. You may need the support of a mental health professional to help you through these obstacles.

How do we meditate?

There are many different approaches to meditation. It has been practiced all over the world for as long as human beings have walked the world. Looking up at the night sky and gazing at the stars, your thoughts may fade away as you ponder their mystery. Simply sitting and looking out over a lake, field or into a forest, you pay special attention to the sounds of birds and animals singing and scampering. Standing above a cityscape, watching it from a skyscraper, you may see the connection between the movement of humans and the stillness of the earth.

You may bring your spiritual practice into your meditation or you may choose to keep it secular. Initially, you will keep it simple: you, your breath and your stillness.

BREATH AWARENESS

A SEAT FOR THE BREATH

To become aware of your breath, it's best to be still, comfortable and away from distractions. Eventually, you may create a special space for your meditation practice.

To begin, simply find a chair. Plant your feet on the floor and bring your spine away from the back of the chair. Let your back be its strong and supple self, lifting out of the seat of your pelvis like a tall tree. Respect its natural curves, the low back, neck and upper back. Let your shoulders move down your back. Rest your hands on your knees or in your lap. Close your eyes.

Notice how you breathe. Feel your belly and chest rise as you breathe in. Feel your belly gently move in toward your spine as you breathe out. Stay with this breathing and find your own easy pace. Keep breathing. No holding. No catching up. Just breathe. In. Out.

You may lose track of time. But sense that you are breathing like this for about five minutes.

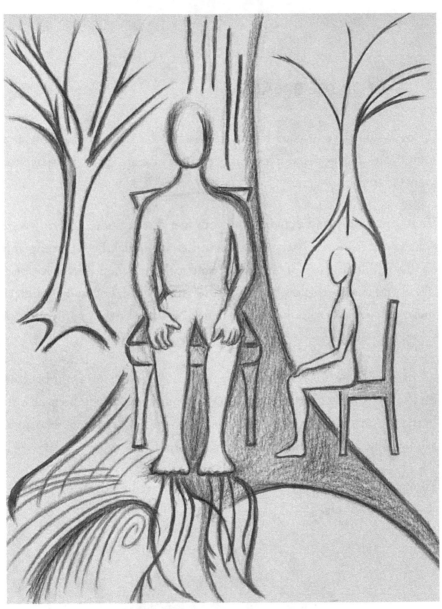

When Heaven and Earth come together they
plant the seed of Thunder in the ground.

SEATED CLOUD HANDS

Establish your comfortable seat for the breath. Take a few breaths to establish your easy pace.

Pick up your hands and extend your forearms, lining them up close to your waist with the elbows just outside of the hips. Be sure that your neck and shoulders are relaxed. Lift your chest just a little.

Your palms are facing into your belly, about a foot in front. Spread the fingers gently apart, as though you are holding a large grapefruit in each hand. Let the fingers be relaxed, open and sensitive to the air around them.

Breathe in. Move your hands apart slowly. Breathe out. Bring them together, also slowly, leaving a volleyball-size space between them. Repeat. Keep breathing and moving the hands together and apart at a steady and relaxed pace. You may start to notice that you can actually feel your hands wrapping around the air as they pass through it.

Continue for 10 full breath cycles, breathing in, breathing out. When you are finished, relax your hands to your lap and sit quietly for as long as you like.

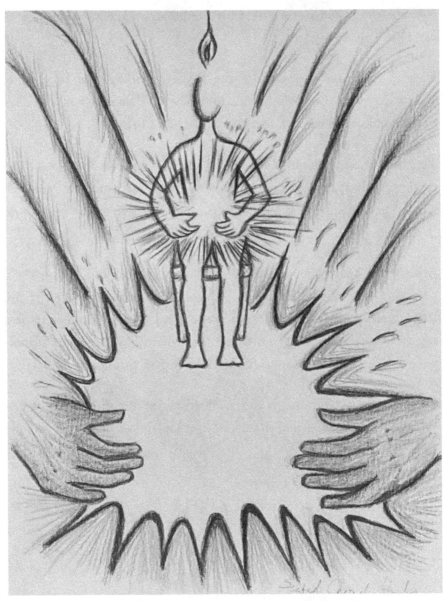

Warmed by Fire and nourished by
Earth, Thunder begins to move.

MOUNTAIN

Stand with your heels directly under your hips. Spread your toes and ball of your foot as wide as you can. Lift your toes and feel the outer edges of your feet and the hollow of the arch. Relax the toes back down and let the whole foot ground or sink heavily into the earth beneath it.

Take your attention to the top of your head. Imagine a string attached there, gently lifting you towards heaven. Feel the back of your neck lengthening and your shoulders releasing down your back. Lift your chest from the center of your back, only a little. Feel your shoulders opening out to the sides and back, making your chest broader. Look down your nose so that your chin lines up with the base of your throat. Gaze forward at a single point that is not moving. This can be an imaginary point.

Straighten your legs without locking out the knees. Contract the muscles all around the legs and the thighs. Contract the inner thigh muscles. Gently pull the belly in below the navel. Maintain a slight tension in all these muscles as you relax and continue to stand.

Breathe in. Let your body expand out to the sides and up and down from head to toe. Breathe out. Let your body relax inward towards the spine and navel.

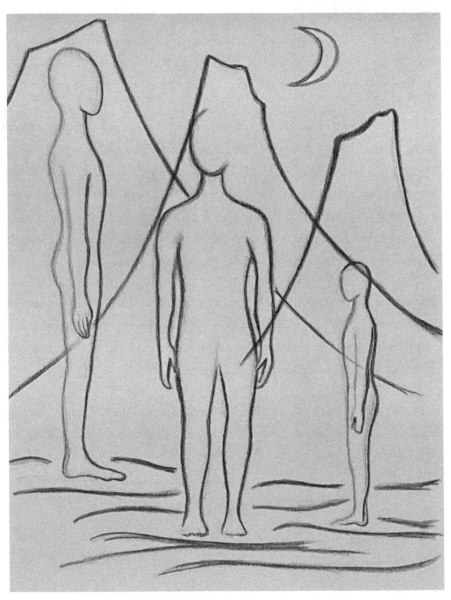

Pushing up through the Earth, Thunder rises to the sky. Mountain stands in its place, tall and still.

WATER MOUNTAIN

Stand in Mountain. Form your Seated Cloud Hands. Change their orientation so that one hand is on top, across from the chest; the other hand is just below the navel. Both palms face the body. Breathe in.

Breathe out. Bend the knees slowly and bring the hands together to pass each other, top hand going down, bottom hand coming up.

Breathe in. Slowly straighten the knees and bring the hands together to pass each other, bottom hand coming up and top hand going down.

Maintain your strong, relaxed Mountain as you bend and straighten, passing your hands by one another like water moving up and down the front of the spine.

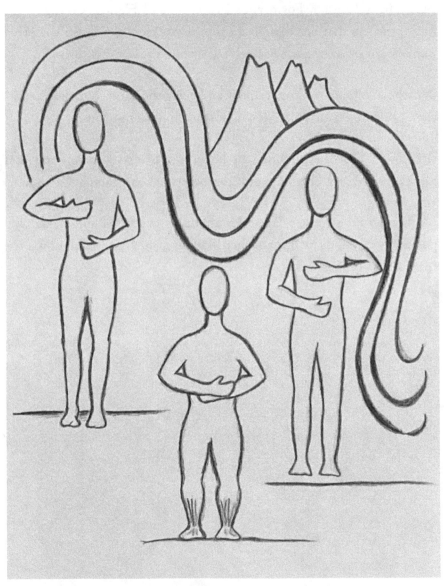

In Heaven, Thunder joins with Water. Together,
they form Lake on top of Mountain.

SHIFTING CLOUD HANDS

Widen your Mountain by stepping out to shoulder width. This is called a horse stance. Keep the toes pointed forward, feet parallel. Form your Cloud Hands, left hand near the heart space, right hand just below the navel. Both palms face the body.

Breathe in and shift your weight to your left leg. Move your bottom hand up and your top hand down.

Breathe out and shift your weight to your right leg. Move your bottom hand up and your top hand down.

Keep the torso strong and balanced on the legs. You're just moving it from one leg to the other. Be loose and relaxed with your hands and your breath.

Be like the clouds drifting in the sky. Let your thoughts disperse like the wind whisks away clouds.

Make adjustments with your feet and arms. Make the movement work for you.

With gentle persistence, Wind penetrates
the hard rock of Earth.

MINDFULNESS

It is natural for your mind to think. However, this thinking can be a source of stress. Consider some of the things you think about --- constantly. Many of the thoughts involve concern for the future and regret or anger over the past. Recall the driver that cut you off on the freeway. Notice how long it takes for that thought to fade.

These worry, anger thoughts have their roots in fear. Your body's response to fear is to go into sympathetic or fight-or-flight mode. This is great when your body actually has something to do, like run or fight for your life. But if this response becomes chronic, it's like anything we overdo. It begins to work against you and your body.

Exercise and meditation can help alleviate a lot of your stress. Both give the body something to do with that fight-or-flight energy and help to dissipate its destructive effects. Meditation helps you to eliminate the effects of stress by calming your mind and body. However, you can still be thinking furiously while you're doing either of these activities. To remove the roots of the stress, you need to go to the thoughts, recognize the effects, and let them go.

Does that mean you're going to solve the ongoing issue? Maybe. But when you finally stop constantly ruminating over the thought, you're in a healthier position, mentally and physically to face the problem.

Mindfulness is a term for this process of paying attention to your thinking.

BELLY BREATH

Take your Seat for the Breath, in a chair or in a crossed-legged or comfortable seat on the floor, or on a cushion on the floor. Learn to sit on the floor for even short periods of time, if you can. This will strengthen your spine and torso as well as keep your hips flexible. Don't worry if you cannot. You will still benefit from this exercise.

Begin to breathe. Establish a comfortable rhythm.

Breathe in. Feel your whole front body expand outward from below the navel to the top of the chest. Breathe out. Let your back body be strong and tall as the front body relaxes into it. Continue this way for a while. Front body expands outward on the inhale. Back body supports front body on the exhale.

Keep the back strong and tall. Breathe in. Fill the front body like a container, from the low belly, mid belly to top of the chest. Breathe out. Empty the front body from the top of the chest to the mid belly to the low belly. Continue for at least ten breaths.

Let the belly breath go and breathe naturally, without thinking about how you do it. Observe your thoughts like fish swimming before you in an aquarium. Notice them. Let them pass by. They will return. In the meantime, enjoy the silence.

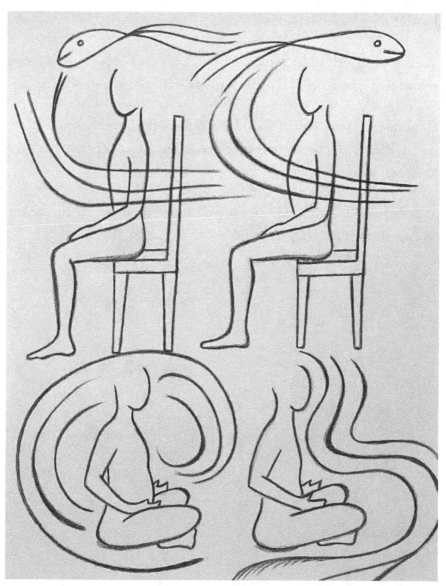

Fire heats Wind. Wind sends Fire roaring over Earth.

OCEAN BREATH

Make a Seat for the Breath. Bring your attention to your breathing. Establish your gentle rhythm.

Breathe in. Lightly constrict your throat to make a hissing or whispering sound as you breathe. Make that same sound again as you breathe out.

Continue to do this for ten to twelve breaths. Breathe in the sound of the ocean. Breathe out the sound of the ocean. Then let the ocean breath go and breathe freely.

Watch your thoughts roll in and roll out like waves on the ocean. Welcome them in. Wave them on.

Earth guides Fire and Wind in the cycle
of destruction and renewal.

OCEAN BREATH SHIFTING CLOUD HANDS

Stand for Shifting Cloud Hands. Hold the hands out in front of you, about a foot from the body. Palms face the body. Top hand is near the chest. Bottom hand is near the navel.

Begin the Ocean Breath. Establish your rhythm.

Breathe in. Shift your weight to the right leg and reach your hands to the right. The arms come parallel to each other. Feel as though you are sweeping away the thoughts that you do not need.

Breathe out. Shift your weight to the left leg. Bring the arms back towards the torso, along with the gift of healing energy to yourself. Reach the arms out to the left. Extend your healing energy into the space around you.

Continue shifting and breathing. Reach the arms out to let go of things you do not want. Bring healing energy in as the arms cross the center of the body. Send healing energy out for yourself and others as your arms pass to the other side. You may do this for a long time.

End by standing in Mountain. Be still.

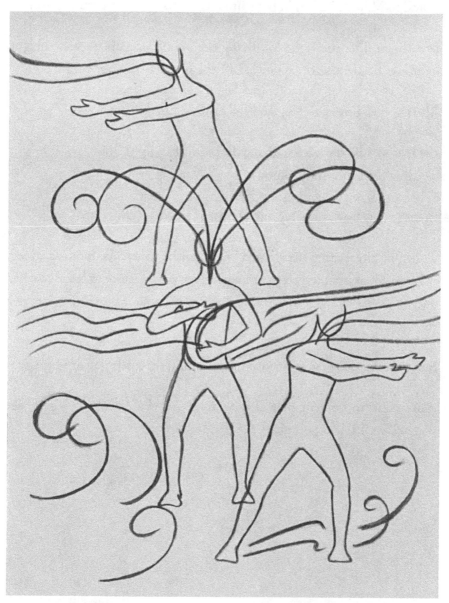

Thunder stirs Lake, the Joyous, to dance upon the Earth.

WALKING IN PLACE

Stand in Mountain. Begin breathing. Establish your breath rhythm.

Breathe in. Lift the right leg. Bring the palms face up to waist height, bending the arms at the elbows. Lift the bones with your mind.

Breathe out. Lower the leg and the arms, palms facing down.

Breathe in. Lift the left leg. Bring the palms face up to about waist height, bending the arms at the elbows.

Breathe out. Lower the leg and the arms, palms facing down.

Continue alternating lifting and lowering the forearms, hands and legs this way for at least ten steps or longer. Practice pausing to balance when one leg is off the ground. Remember to breathe, following your own rhythm.

Stand in the stillness of Mountain or sit quietly when you are finished.

Note: This movement may also be done in a chair. Lift the legs or see yourself walking as you move the hands.

Wind sends ripples over the smiling Lake.

WALKING FORWARD, WALKING BACKWARD

Stand in Mountain. Establish your breathing rhythm.

Form an energy ball (also called a tai chi ball) with your right hand on top, palm down, chest level. Your left hand is palm up at the navel. Stand on your right leg, keeping the left toes on the floor.

Step forward with your left foot. Turn your ball over. Left hand is palm down at chest level. Right hand is palm up at the navel.

Take two more steps forward, turning the ball over each time.

Then step the left foot backward, turn your ball over and stand on the left leg.

Step the right foot backward, turn your ball over and stand on the right leg. Take two more steps backward.

Continue in this way for as long as you like, taking four steps forward and four steps backward. Remember to breathe with your natural rhythm. Let go of any perceived mistakes. Concentrate on one movement at a time. Follow every step of the movement with your mind.

End by standing in Mountain or sitting quietly.

Note: If you are in a chair, move the arms and legs as you are able and use your mind to see yourself doing the movement.

Mountain shifts slowly back and forth
like Water lapping the shore.

SELF-CALMING

As adults, most of us are able to control our negative emotions around others, if only for the sake of getting things done. However, these negative emotions repeatedly find ways to show up in our thinking and behavior. They seem completely irrational. They're rooted in the past. If we ignore them, they find ways to get our attention. We develop habits, patterns of thinking and behaving that hold us back from growing into happy humans being.

With mindfulness practice, you noticed your thinking. With self-calming, you will pay attention to your emotions. Negative emotions will come up in your thinking as you are meditating. This is a good time to become free of them, while you are calm.

Let the positive emotions linger as long as they stay. You want them to be the norm. It's the destructive emotions, the ones that make you feel bad, that you want to release from your life.

Do not fight the negative emotions. They will only fight back. Simply acknowledge them and then let them go. I used the word simply because I know how hard it is. Like everything, it takes consistent practice.

NAME THAT EMOTION

Come to your Seat for the Breath. You may be in a chair or seated comfortably on the floor. In either place, let your spine be self-supported or comfortably supported.

Breathe with awareness. Feel yourself expand on the in breath. Relax the body as you breathe out. Maintain your tall spine. Keep the chest slightly lifted and the chin slightly lowered. Feel yourself moving deeper into your heart space, a place of safety, peace and love. Continue this breath pattern until you feel mentally quiet.

When you notice a negative emotion rise out of a thought or feeling, just name it. Examples are: anger, jealousy, hatred, desiring or wanting, superiority, inferiority, criticism, judgment, or fear. After naming the negative emotion, go back to your meditation. Be alert for the next one to arrive or for a return of the last one. Name it, let it go and continue with your breathing.

After a while, let go of the activity and sit quietly.

Fire brightly burns up the debris of
fear that smothers the heart.

CAT-COW

This movement can be done seated on a chair, starting from your Seat for the Breath. It can also be done standing, supporting yourself by placing your hands on the chair, either the back of the chair or the seat, depending on your flexibility. With more flexibility and strength, you can do this on a yoga mat, on your hands and knees, in a table top position.

Assuming you are in a chair, take a breath in and lift your chest. Feel a bit of a backbend between your shoulder blades, at the bottom of the rib cage. Keep your head and neck in line with the spine. There should be a nice arch in your back. Lift your tailbone high. This is <u>Cow</u>. The back is shaped like a bowl receiving.

When you breathe out, move your spine in the opposite direction. Round out your spine. Pull your belly in. Curl your head down and under. The low back is rounded forward, tailbone reaching for crown of the head. Keep the shoulders relaxed. This is <u>Cat</u>. The back is shaped like a bowl emptying.

Keep moving this way for 5-10 full breath cycles, breathing in and out. Breathe in and arch to Cow. Breathe out and round to Cat. Name any negative emotions that come up. Let them roll off your back.

When you are finished, sit comfortably with the spine tall and free. Breathe easily. Enjoy the stillness.

Wind bends and extends the spine, squeezing
out blocks of pain from the past.

BODY CHECK

When you feel your emotions racing out of control in a situation, your best response is to breathe. Just tell yourself that. Breathe. Since you've been practicing, you should be able to do this right away. You don't have to look cool and calm. Just breathe and wait 3-5 breaths before you act. Give your brain some oxygen. Give yourself a chance to be creative. This will take some practice but if you do practice, it will become second nature. Try practicing now.

Stand in Mountain. This can also be done sitting or lying down. In the beginning, standing, if possible, helps you focus better. Close your eyes. Breathe. After 5 breaths, recall or let come to you, a person or situation that causes you to react with less control than you would like. Notice how this reaction makes you feel and where this feeling is located in the body. Maybe your heart beats faster, your throat constricts or your head or stomach hurts.

Once you've established where the emotion is located, use your mind to comfort and release it. Visualize that you are breathing peace into that area of your body. Be creative. You may not always be able to find the emotion in a particular area of the body. In that case, simply practice breathing peace into your whole body.

When you feel that your body is in a place of balance, turn your attention to the person or situation that distressed you. Breathe peace to yourself on your inhale. Breathe peace out to the person or situation on the exhale.

Breathe peace until you feel peace. Slowly open your eyes.

In stillness, Mountain is cleansed by
Water and warmed by Fire.

HEART OPENER

Create a bolster out of one or two blankets folded to support your spine. It's best to do this on the floor and with something firm, like blankets or a yoga bolster. But you can do this on your bed and use a firm pillow or two. You may also want a blanket or pillow to support your head and neck, whether on the bed or the floor.

Sit with your sacrum against the bolster and lie back onto it. You may have to adjust yourself a few times before you are completely comfortable. Your arms should drape off the sides of the bolster so that you feel your chest opening upward and outward slightly. If you are able, bend your elbows, leaving your whole arm on the floor. Your arms will form a cactus shape. If this is uncomfortable, leave your arms straight and closer to your sides. You may bend your knees or let your legs be straight, let your feet be wide apart or close together.

Begin to breathe consciously. Deepen your breath, making the inhale just a little longer and the exhale a little slower, without straining. Notice the heart space in the center of the chest. Imagine the in breath filling your heart space. Let the out breath flow into your whole body.

Do this for 5 minutes. Keep breathing through any emotions that surface.

When you are finished, bend your knees and gently roll to one side, supporting yourself with your arms. Slowly and gently push yourself up to sit comfortably. Stay here for a while.

Heaven blossoms from the peaceful heart of Earth.

WARRIOR

Stand in Mountain. Take a few breaths here.

Step the right leg out to the right as far as you can and still maintain a balanced posture.

Check to make sure your heels are on the same line, if you were to draw a line behind them. If you want support for balance, you can stand near a wall or hold onto a chair with one hand. You can even do this sitting in a chair, with a few adjustments.

Turn your right foot 90 degrees and turn your left foot in about 45 degrees. Open your arms straight out over your legs. Bend your right knee as deep as you can and still see your toes.

Strengthen the left leg and lengthen the left arm in opposition to the forward movement of the right leg and right arm.

Gaze over your right fingertips. Move your right hip back and your left hip forward, squaring them to look in the direction of your gaze.

Notice your breath as you come into this position. Once you are in Warrior, begin the Ocean Breath. Be here for 3-5 breath cycles. Feel and acknowledge your strength and ability to overcome obstacles.

Move in reverse slowly to return to Mountain. Be still. Breathe.

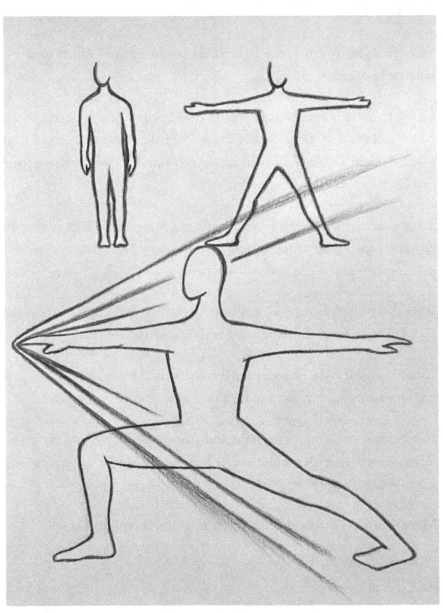

Lake focuses her joy to pierce her goal.

CONCENTRATION

With consistent, focused meditation, you develop stronger concentration. With better mental focus, you will be aware of areas of your life that you want to change or improve. Because you are giving your mind and body conscious relaxation, you are giving yourself space to solve problems creatively, improve your own health and improve your relationships. This will happen as a natural consequence of your consistent practice.

The following meditative movement activities are based on the first three sections: Breath Awareness, Mindfulness and Self-Calming. They expand upon the movements in those sections and the element of concentration.

The first three meditations are combinations of movements you have practiced before. Even though you have already practiced these movements, please do them as described. It is important that you keep track of the number of breaths and that you transition to the next movement as directed. This will help you stay focused and on task while you are in a relaxed state.

The recommended time to stay on each individual movement of the first three series of movements is 6 breath cycles. If this is too long, start with 3 breath cycles for each individual movement. Remember, a breath cycle is a breath in and a breath out.

If you find you are able to go up to 12 breath cycles for each individual movement, you are doing very well. In that case, you may, with awareness, begin to mix and match different movements according to your inclination.

Add more awareness to your movements by consciously transitioning in an easy and relaxed manner from one movement to the next.

Find detailed descriptions of the movements in the previous sections of the book. It may take awhile to piece the meditations together. But this work is all part of the practice of concentration and creation.

CONCENTRATION COMBINATION 1

Seat for the Breath (Breath Awareness), **Ocean Breath** (Mindfulness), **Cat-Cow** (Self-Calming)

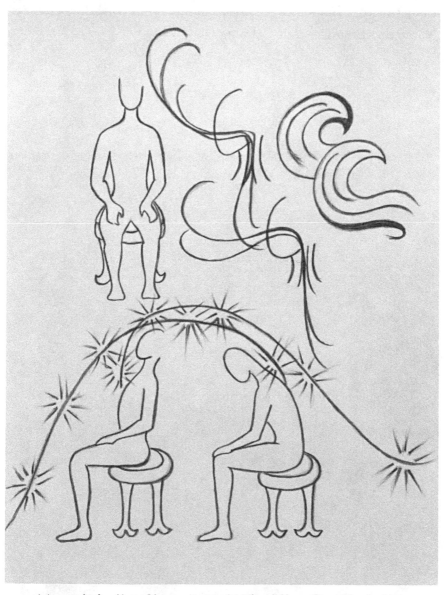

Mountain the Strong and Wind the Gentle bring
Fire the Clinging to a soft, steady glow.

CONCENTRATION COMBINATION 2

Belly Breath (Mindfulness), **Seated Cloud Hands** (Breath Awareness), **Name that Emotion** (Self-Calming)

Fire shimmers over Water, brightening
the night sky of Heaven.

CONCENTRATION COMBINATION 3

Mountain (Breath Awareness), **Body Check** (Self-Calming), **Ocean Breath, Shifting Cloud Hands** (Mindfulness)

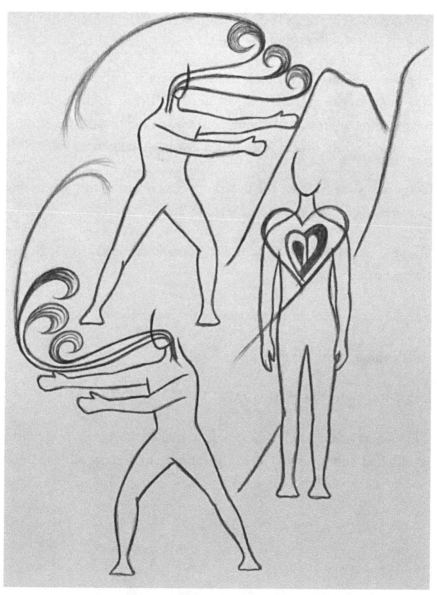

Buffeted by Wind and Fire, Mountain
stands clear and bright.

ALTERNATE NOSTRIL BREATHING

This is a yoga breath exercise. Practicing it brings balance to mind and body. It also requires concentration.

There is a version where you can use your right hand, thumb, middle and ring finger to close off the nostrils. Let's use the more difficult, subtle version. Simply breathe in through one nostril and breathe out through the other. Feel the breath. Visualize it as a healing light.

Come into your Seat for the Breath. Begin breathing through both of your nostrils for three or more breath cycles.

On your next inhale, see and feel the breath coming in through your right nostril.

Exhale: see and feel the breath leaving through your left nostril.

Inhale through the left nostril.

Exhale through the right.

This counts as one round of alternate nostril breathing. Start off with 4 rounds and work your way up to eight. End your practice with an inhale and exhale through both nostrils.

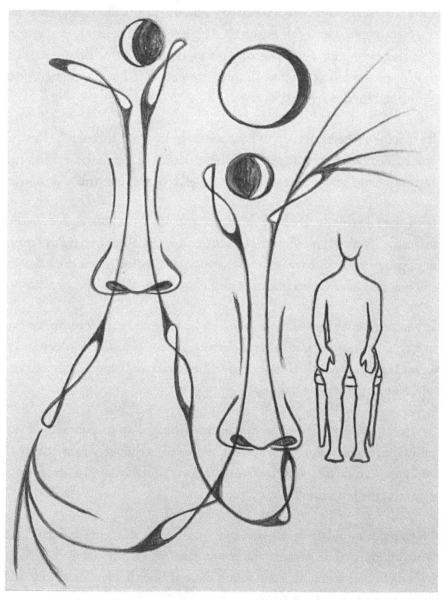

Water passes through all the high
and low spaces of Earth.

YOGA NIDRA

This is a yoga meditation practice that could also be called yoga sleep. It's the fact that you don't fall asleep that makes it a concentration exercise. You come very close, so close that it's even more restful than sleep. It's that in-between waking and sleeping time, that delicious moment just before you finally drift off to sleep.

It's helpful in the beginning to have someone lead you through it. Restful guided meditation apps on your cell phone may serve this purpose. But since you are practicing concentration, you will lead yourself into this state of rest.

It's best to do this on a mat on the floor. You can put a bolster under your knees and give your neck and head a little support. You can have a blanket over you or you can have none of these. Spread your legs to the edges of the mat and have your arms out from your sides, palms up.

If you cannot lay on the floor, you can lie on your bed. You can also sit in a chair. Wherever you are, stay awake. Of course, falling asleep is not a bad thing, especially if you need it. But practice being deeply relaxed and enjoying it with awareness.

Settle in, close your eyes and start breathing. Say to yourself, "I am practicing Yoga Nidra now." Speak to yourself as though you are the wise and gentle guide into your own meditation. You may eventually want to create a tape of yourself.

Notice the sounds around you, beginning with the sounds outside of your building, then outside the room, then inside the room. Let these sounds fade as you notice the sound of your breath, your heartbeat and other sounds from your body.

Let go of the outside sounds, the body sounds and notice the noise of the thoughts in your mind. Use the breath to help you let the thoughts drift away until they are relatively quiet.

This is a good point at which to set an intention, a goal or purpose. You might say, "I am grateful that I am in this present moment", or "I am grateful to be healthy", or "I am grateful for my joy-filled relationships".

Bring your awareness to your body. You will relax it with your mind. Begin with the fingers of your right hand. Say, "Relax, fingers of my right hand." Move to your arm and shoulder. Do the same on the Left hand and arm. Next, go to the right toes and foot, leg and thigh. Do the same for the left side. Take your time. Be detailed. Linger. Feel your body releasing heavily into the mat, bit by bit.

Relax your glutes, pelvis, hips, low back, mid-back, upper back, neck, head, face, throat, chest, and belly. Once you've individually relaxed the parts of your body, relax the whole body. Say "Relax, my whole body." Say this as many times as feels right.

Lay here and enjoy the relaxation while staying awake. At this time, you may want to bring more attention and healing thoughts to specific areas of your body. You may want to practice alternate nostril breathing or ocean breath to maintain your focus. You may find that it's enough to simply enjoy the peace.

You may be here for 5 minutes or longer. Twenty minutes is a good start.

When you are ready to end, you can repeat the intention, goal or gift you gave to yourself in the beginning of your practice. In these relaxed states, intentions sink deeply and effectively into the consciousness, so be mindful with the feelings that surround them.

Breathe deeply. Stretch gently. Then bend your knees and roll to your side. Linger here for a breath or two. Slowly come up to sit. Be still and breathe.

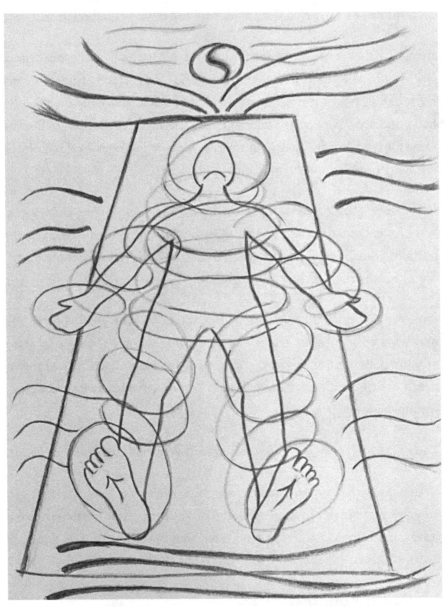

Wind and Water carry the quiet
Mountain over the ocean of bliss.

SELF-KNOWLEDGE

Knowing others is wisdom;
Knowing the self is enlightenment.
Mastering others requires force;
Mastering the self requires strength;
He who knows he has enough is rich.
Perseverance is a sign of will power.

-- Lao Tsu

If you have been practicing any of the above activities on a regular basis, you may already be experiencing self-knowledge. You will recognize this positive adventure as an "Aha" moment or a feeling of coming home -- to yourself, the one you always knew was there but somehow had forgotten. Self-knowledge is the jewel in the heart of your meditation practice. It is the source of the power you express in the world.

We were born with awareness of our potential for greatness. Unfortunately, some of our experiences in the world caused us to doubt this potential and to create defenses to support ourselves instead. These defenses keep us from experiencing the joy of being who we really are.

Who you really are is a personal gift you give to yourself. It is not what other people are, so there's no need to report to others or to compare your experience with them. It's not something you can decide to be. That's one of the false defenses. It's something that's always there and comes to you when you are open to it. It is fluid and brings freedom to your movements.

This gift of self-knowledge can come to you at any time. But regular, consistent meditation practice is the perseverance that fuels the process.

Meditative movement now includes activities that you are drawn to. These are things you may suddenly find you have been doing for a long time, so involved in the present that you lose track of time.

The following activities address attitudes and thought processes more deeply than previous exercises in this book. They are only a small sample. Use them to help you explore and develop your own ways of self-knowing.

FACING YOUR FEARS

Come to your Seat for the Breath. This is a comfortable seat of your choosing. If it's easy, keep the spine free and unsupported. Bring your awareness to your breath.

Raise your right hand, palm facing outward, fingertips upward, near your right shoulder.

Lower your left hand, palm facing outward, fingertips downward, between the navel and the hip.

Both hands are slightly in front of the torso.

Breathe the Ocean Breath. Whenever a fear arises, bring your awareness to your right hand and send the fear away. Then bring your attention to your left hand to receive the blessings of peace.

You may breathe the Ocean Breath for 12 full breaths in and out. Then let that go and breathe easily and quietly. Hold this gesture of sending away fears and receiving the blessings of peace for as long as you like.

When you are finished, bring your palms together at your heart and bow your head slightly, in a gesture of honor and respect for yourself and the universe.

Fire and Heaven watch over Lake as
she repels fear and offers peace.

FORGIVENESS

If you are holding a grudge against someone else or feeling anger at a situation, this can keep you from being in the present moment and from enjoying your own company. Forgiveness must be practiced. The following exercise may help you do that.

Establish a horse stance, feet shoulder width apart and parallel, knees slightly bent. Step the left foot forward one footstep. Keep the foot parallel with the right one. Turn the right foot out about 45 degrees. Shift your weight to the right leg. Keep your hips and spine upright.

Shift your weight forward to the left foot, arms and palms reaching away from you.

Shift your weight back to the right foot, arms and palms coming back into your heart space.

Weight to the left foot: palms and arms opening away from you.

Weight to the right foot: palms and arms returning into your heart space.

Feel as though you are letting go of your anger and filling your heart with love and compassion. Even if you don't actually feel this way, practicing the gesture may open a way of real forgiveness for you.

When you have done 10 shifts back and forth switch legs. Now the right leg is in front and parallel. The left foot is turned out to 45 degrees. Remember to keep a shoulder width between your feet. Start with your weight over the left foot.

Shift forward to release and forgive. Shift backward to receive love and compassion.

When you are finished, stand quietly in Mountain for a few breaths.

Thunder and Wind rock Mountain to
shake out the obstructions to love.

ASPIRATIONS

When you were very young, you may have had hopes and dreams without limits. Anything was possible. Perhaps as you became older, you learned to stash those dreams away. Peers may have laughed at you. Parents may have helped you reason them away. So your aspirations stayed in the realm of dreams.

Now it's time to have some fun. Be a child again and draw some pictures of yourself as that astronaut or dancer or doctor. Make a list of things you love or love to do. Write a story, poem or song of yourself, being, doing, one of your dreams. Let all limitations fall away. Be in the universe of infinite possibilities.

Create a meditative movement to honor one of your cherished dreams. Draw on what you have learned in this book or make up a movement of your own. Keep it simple, rhythmic and enjoyable. Two moves are enough. Be the aspiration. Breathe in the dream. Exhale and let it flow through your body and limbs.

End your meditative movement with a few moments of stillness. Bring your hands together at your heart and thank the dream.

Carried by Wind, Lake the Joyous is lifted
to Heaven by Thunder and Fire.

AFFIRMATIONS

Remember that just as a tree doesn't grow in a day, week, season or year, but gradually, over time, your progress toward self-knowledge is also a result of consistent practice and attention. You are changing the way you think about and talk to yourself.

No doubt you've noticed that most of us are our own worst critics. Noticing and quieting the inner critic is one way to change how we relate to ourselves. Another way is to cultivate your own inner cheerleader. Affirmations are your cheers.

An affirmation is a statement establishing the truth of something. Examples are: I am happy; I am healthy; I am prosperous. Gratitude is a naturally positive state of mind. So if you put the words, I am grateful at the start of your affirmation, it becomes doubly affirming. I am grateful that I am happy is a statement that connects your happiness to the Universe.

There is no one way to make affirmations. You can find many sources to help you. Eventually, you will find your own way.

For the following affirmation movement, use this statement:

I am grateful I am healthy.

Stand in a very wide horse stance, legs spread apart more than shoulder width. Turn your feet out to slight diagonals.

As you breathe in, reach your arm up and out in a V shape. This is Star Pose, which is appropriate because you are a star.

Breathe out, bend your knees and bring your hands together at your heart, a symbol of honor and respect for yourself and the universe. Say to yourself: I am grateful.

Breathe in. Straighten your legs and reach your arms up to the V. Say to yourself: I am healthy.

Continue this affirmation movement for five or more breath cycles. Use ocean breath and speak the affirmation silently.

When you are finished, stand in mountain for a few quiet breaths and relish the effects of this gift of positive thought to yourself.

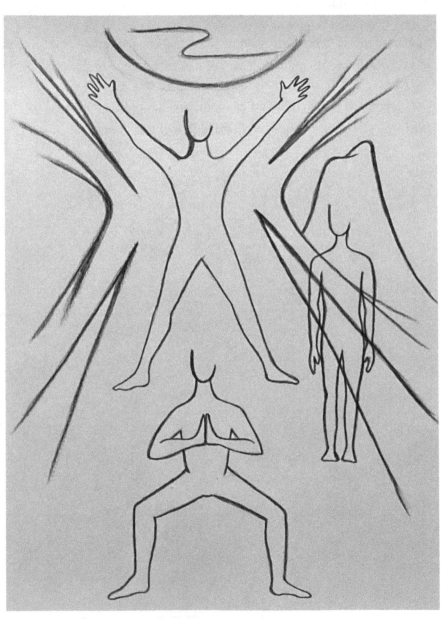

Water and Thunder rise above Mountain
and rain refreshes Earth.

HEALING

In the universe, difficult things are done as if they are easy.
In the universe great acts are made up of small deeds.

--- Lao Tsu

As stated in the beginning of this book, relaxation in itself contributes to healing. By consistently taking the time to breathe with awareness, you are contributing to your own healing. By endeavoring to search and root out the emotions that block your way to healing, you are making yourself well. There are many sources that can help you with self-healing. Here is another.

Pick one or more of the standing or sitting movements with arm and/or leg motions from the previous sections. Use these to warm up the body and slow down the mind. Connect with your breath here.

After your warm up, take your Seat for the Breath. Breathe easily, smoothly and deeply. Cultivate the feeling of ease and relaxation. Release the tension in your mind and on your face. You are doing nothing, wanting nothing, only being. Stay here for as long as you like or continue on with the next part of this meditation.

See with your inner eye the part of your body, mind or life you would like to heal. Connect with any emotions aroused by this image. This may not happen the first time you try it. However, if you feel ready to face any emotions that arise or if you are sure they are there but have not surfaced yet, keep returning to this activity over time. Let it be easy. Let it come naturally.

If you are ready to face any emotions that arise in connection with your dis-ease, use your analytic mind to learn about them. Go forward when it is easy. Retreat when it becomes difficult. Use the breath to stay present and detached as you explore and eventually release this emotion. Stay here as long as you need or continue on with the next part of the meditation.

See with your inner eye that you are completely healed of your dis-ease. Accept and be with this image. Stay with your breath, knowing that it connects you to the Universe. Let go of any need to achieve, own or be this image. Let it happen. Stay here in effortless peace for as long as you like before slowly coming out of your meditation.

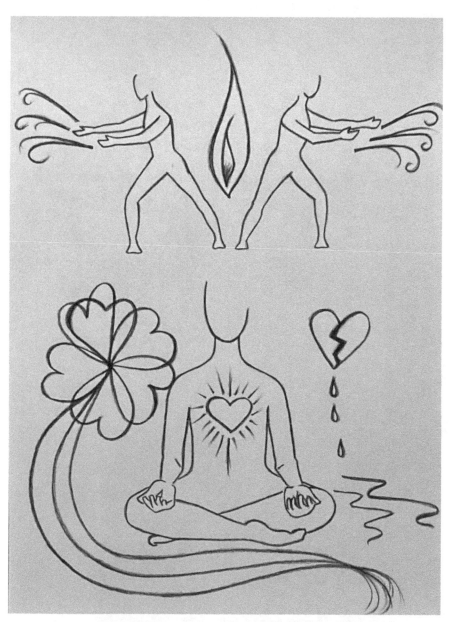

The family of Heaven and Earth, Thunder and
Water, Wind and Fire, Mountain and Lake join
to create the balanced heart and mind.

BIBLIOGRAPHY

Success Through Stillness, Meditation Made Simple, Russell Simmons with Chris Morrow, 2014

Secular Meditation, Rick Heller, 2015

The Art of Happiness, His Holiness, The Dalai Lama and Howard C. Cutler, M.D., 1998

Stages of Meditation, The Dalai Lama, translated by Venerable Geshe Lobsang Jordhen, Losang Choephel Ganchenpa, and Jeremy Russell, 2001

The Fine Arts of Relaxation, Concentration and Meditation, Joel & Michelle Levy, Wisdom Publications, 2003

Meditation for the Love of It, Sally Kempton, Sounds True, Inc., 2011

Meditation for Optimum Health, Andrew Weil and John Kabat-Zinn, Sounds True, Inc., 2001

How to Relax, Thich Nhat Hahn, Parallax Press, 2015

Yoga Nidra, Swami Satyananda Saraswati, 1976

Meditation Teacher Training Program, Tara Cindy Sherman, 2016

7 Benefits of a Daily Affirmation Plan. The Chopra Center. chopra.com

www.psychologytoday.com/blog/in-love-and-war/201207/the-dangers-self-forgiveness-and-how-avoid-them Juliana Breines Phd

Catherine Ayano Nixon

http://www.mayoclinic.org/healthy-lifestyle/adult-health/in-depth/
forgiveness/art-20047692 Forgiveness: Letting Go of Grudges and
Bitterness

<u>Real Relief from Back Pain</u>, Consumer Reports, June 2017